# DECOUPAGE

## For beginners.

Simple **DECOUPAGE**

Projects (Step by step Guide).

By

Dr. Janet Willie.

# Table of Contents.

# CHAPTER 1.

## INTRODUCTION TO THE ART OF DECOUPAGE.

Decoupage is a specialty technique that involves attaching paper-like decorations to a surface that is usually hard, using glue. It started in France around the 17th century, and it is sometimes considered as an alternative to painted furniture. This technique is very simple to learn, as most objects that are made from wood or other materials are engraved with patterns that are drawn from magazines or newspapers.

It involves applying several coats of paint to a surface. The goal is to make it appear as if it wasn't stuck on. With this technique, you can create various designs for various objects in your possession. The finished product can make a great impression on others, and it's a great method to revitalize worn out furniture. It can also be utilized to make designs for various occasions, such as Easter and Christmas.

Decoupage as a word originates from the verb *Découper*, in French, meaning "to cut out". Applying this technique, you can customize practically anything in your possession and interestingly, the designs can be as basic or as complex as you prefer.

The completed work can look so delightful that it gives off an impression of being expertly painted. You can decoupage basically anything in your home, and it's an extraordinary method to refresh or tidy up furniture that is looking somewhat worn. It can likewise be used to make designs suitable for decorations for great occasions like that of Easter by beautifying and creating patterns on eggs, or used during Christmas for making tree decorations.

Decoupage is a relaxing, and entertaining style of art that may be done by people of all ages and abilities. Therefore you can renovate your household objects by giving them a fresh outlook, or create something lovely and adorning for your home. There are so many things you can buy for the sole purpose of decoupage, but the amazing thing about this art is that you might possibly have some of these items or materials needed to start up the process in your home. All you'll need to get started are a few basic materials and instruments like scissors, a craft blade, wrapping paper, paper napkins or magazines.

Decoupage is a mild painting form that can transform any surface into something beautiful with just a few scraps of paper or fabric. Decoupage derived from the French phrase découper, meaning "to carve off or cut out." It's a simple and enjoyable art and it is not as difficult as it appears. So many persons might have heard about it but without an idea of what it's all about or maybe it's your first time of getting to know about it. Anyways, you have absolutely nothing to worry about!

Let's begin with its history, the necessary materials that are needed, where to find them and a step-by-step instruction with some starting tips you need to know.

# WHAT'S DECOUPAGE?

Decoupage is simply an art style in which various paper or fabric pieces are glued on the surface of vessels, jewelry cases, wooden slabs, or other furniture objects to give them a fancy and attractive appearance. Oftentimes, papers are more preferable compare to fabrics because of cost, accessibility with less effort. Cut-outs from magazines, posters, printed papers, wrapping papers, and even tissue sheets can be used. Decoupage as an art can be used to customize practically any object in your home, and the best part is that the designs can be as basic or as tricky as you want them to be.

# CHAPTER 2

## HISTORICAL BACKGROUND OF DECOUPAGE.

Decoupage has a rich history that has been impacted by many countries. This kind of art was previously known as a paper cutting method before gaining popularity in France. East Siberia is thought to be where decoupage began, with nomadic clans making patted cut-outs to decorate the dead's burial chambers. This process then spread to China via Siberia, and by the 12th-century, perforated papers were being used to decorate lamps, windows, e-boxes, and other items.

Trades between Venice and the Far East flourished in the 17th-century, and decoupage spread throughout Europe as a result of these links. Coating paper patterns onto bookshelves, cupboards, and other furniture or things for decoration became popular here. Decoupage quickly became popular throughout Europe, and it became a sought-after design. It became a fashionable pastime, especially among the Italian, French, and English courts. Effortless, captivating, and attractive designs were fastened on fans, screens, and bathroom products using photographs already printed specifically for this art form.

Decoupage was used to create peep shows and miniature scenes that could be seen via a small opening in the nineteenth century. During the Victorian era, amazing decoupage artwork began to appear all over the place. Decoupage lessons were given to young ladies as a way to beautify objects, and scraping projects were displayed.

Despite the fact that decoupage has been dormant for a long time, it was revived in the twentieth century by Americans looking to preserve montages and invigorate equipment. Many people today decoupage their phone cases, ornaments, napkins, wine bottles, and other items. While it was formerly a strategy used only by skilled craftsmen, it is now a very well-known specialty.

# CHAPTER 3.

## ITEMS NEEDED FOR DECOUPAGE.

Decoupage requires the use of some basic materials. It's a one-of-a-kind art style that demands a plethora of additional materials to polish the piece and give it a great finishing. These items include;

- A platform / surface to decoupage on
- Prints or cut-outs to decoupage with
- Glue
- Sealer
- Paintbrush
- Brayer
- Acrylic paint
- Napkin or tissue paper
- Scissors or craft knife
- Cutting board / mat

☐ *Prints or Cut-outs To Decoupage With*:

Virtually any type of paper can be used. Although is easier to glue thin papers because thicker pieces may be more difficult to stick to the surface as they may require more time and glue. Decoupage with tissue papers on the other hand, is easier to paste and takes less time to dry.

You can always get tissue papers created specially for decoupage arts. Specialty and artistic paper may be available in craft stores for your projects. You can even decoupage with prints from old books, magazines, or posters. You can also check out used bookstores for outdated visuals. I frequently save photographs from magazines, posters, and sometimes newspapers that I cut out and keep for later use. You can also use textiles, but for novices, papers are preferred. Even decoupage can be done using napkins.

☐ *Glue:*

Decoupage is best done with PVA (Polyvinyl acetate) glue. It sticks to paper, cards, fabric, wood, and even metals perfectly leaving a dry, transparent end product. There is also unique decoupage glue that is comparable to PVA glue except for regularity. Spray glue is also available, and it dries very quickly. It would be prudent to select particular glue based on your competence level. Although, PVA is the best choice for novices. These glues are available in hardware and craft stores.

## ☐ *Sealer:*

The sealer is used to give the art work a good final touch. Depending on the type of paint material used, it can be shiny of dull in appearance.

## ☐ *Modge Pod*

To give your artwork a wonderful final touch, you won't need glue or sealer if you use Mod Podge because it is a two-in-one product. It has a great non-shiny finishing and may be used for a wide range of crafts.

Mod Podge is a flexible glue that is a must-have for crafters. It is readily available in different varieties; glossy, sparkle, satin, old, dull, etc.

## Paint Brush And Brayer:

The paintbrush is used for applying glue on the surface and gum the print, while a brayer is used to smoothen the end and ensure that a completely smooth surface is obtained.

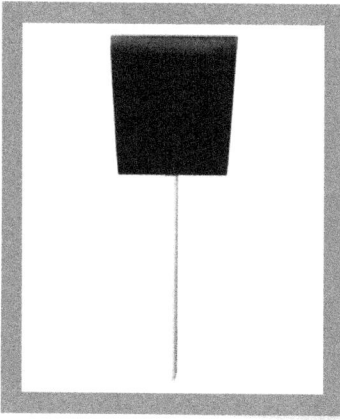

## Napkin or Tissue Paper:

A napkin or tissue paper might be needed to clean off glue from the excessive points.

## Scissors or Craft Knife:

In other to cut out the prints and shape them in accordance with the surface shape, a scissors or craft knife is required.

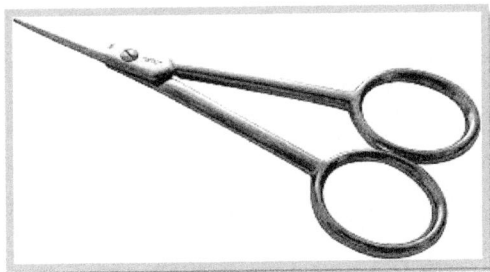

□ *Cutting Board or Mat*:

It's not necessary to use a cutting board or mat. Although it can be used to keep the glue off your table and to determine the size of the print based on your needs.

A cutting board is only useful when you cut frequently while doing your arts and crafts. This mat has a double-sided, self-sealing 5-plywood surface. If you need it, there are measurements along the side to guide you.

# CHAPTER 4.

## BEGINNERS STEP BY STEP GUIDE TO DECOUPAGE.

Now that you know what supplies you'll need, let's talk about how you'll get started!

- **Get your surface ready:** Make sure the surface you've chosen is clean and dry before using it.

- **Arrange your prints in the correct order:** Before applying the glue, resize your prints by laying them on the surface. Arrange them on the surface to make sure you know where to paste them.

- **Place the prints on the surface and glue them:** Apply the glue bit by bit to the surface before sticking your prints.

- Haven glued your prints; give it some time to dry properly. Don't neglect this step if want a good final product

- **Apply a coat of paint to the prints:** Paint the surfaces appropriately section by section after the glue has dried up properly. This will give the surface a gleaming or matte outlook.

♦ **Wait for it to dry:** Yes, you're on your way. Patiently wait for the paint to dry off properly.

You may now use this gorgeous decoupage piece to decorate your apartment.

# CHAPTER 5.

# DECORATIONS YOU CAN MAKE WITH DECOUPAGE.

☐ *Things You Can Decoupage:*

You can decoupage on virtually any object; metal sheets, wooden platforms, cardboards, containers or even glasses. There's absolutely no limit to what you can decoupage with.

♦ Shelves

♦ Drawers/Cabinets

♦ Books

♦ Chairs

♦ Wall Decor

♦ Frames

♦ Glass Containers.

♦ Tables.

♦ Candles.

♦ Bird houses.

♦ Terracotta Pots.

♦ Lamps.

Decoupage can be used on a variety of mediums. It is most commonly used on furniture, containers, mirrors, hardcover books, photo frames boxes, bags, suitcases, dishes, candles, jars, bottles, pebbles, and photograph collections etc. These items may already be in your possession, but you might just want to alter them, or they may have been purchased specifically for decoupage.

Before commencing your decoupage process, the objects you need are those objects you want to customize and the pictures you want to use as well. The use of wood as a decoupage surface is very popular. It's important to note that all you need is to have the correct glue in your possession.

Also, materials such as glass, metals, and plastic can be utilized. As a beginner, you can start with easier items such as bottles or plates. Although, that shouldn't be an issue because you can decoupage almost any material or object in your home. The photographs and designs you utilize for your project might come from almost anywhere. Tissue paper, themes, wrapping papers, postcards, paper napkins, wallpapers, travel pamphlets, programs, paper doilies, book pages, lace, etc.

# CHAPTER 6.

## BASIC TECHNIQUES IN DECOUPAGE.

♣ *Getting Started On Decoupage Project.*
With decoupage, you can achieve some sort of style alteration in your home and make fantastic gifts! The fantastic art technique is suitable for artists of all skill levels, and you can customize each artwork by choosing from a large selection of papers with attractive patterns.

Create layers of patterned sheets to revitalize your tasks or objects. It's quite simple to get started. Decoupaging isn't a difficult craft to master, but it does require time. The good thing about this craft is that you won't have to spend a lot of money to get started, and you won't need to be an expert in the field of creativity to give it a shot. It's best to begin with something simple and straightforward. Purchase suitable surfaces and begin practicing. After gathering all your materials together, you may start working on your project using the steps below as a guide.

♣ *Prepare the Surface:* A decoupage project can be made on almost any surface. Glass, wood, cardboard, or papier-mâché are examples of appropriate surfaces that can be used for decoupage. Plastics are also good, although only a few varieties are suggested. Before you start to work on your project, it is good you test the surface you want to use.

This will help you know if the mod podge or decoupage substance will stick properly. After choosing the item you want to decorate, inspect the surface to ensure it is clean because the paint will always bring out any error on the surface.

♣ _**Prepare your Mod Podge items:**_ Here are a few points to keep in mind before you begin;

● **Fabric:**
   — Wash and dry the fabric thoroughly.
   — Don't even think of using softeners. You can iron it if necessary, or spread it out on a work area.
   — Cover the surface with wax paper if possible.
   — Paint a light layer of Fabric Mod Podge onto your fabric using a good brush and allow it to

air dry. This allows you to cut through cloth without wearing out the edges, just like paper.

♦ **Paper:** Some materials, such as thicker sheets and scrapbooks, can be utilized straight from the package with Mod Podge. Peradventure you are using a slender scrapbook paper sheets or inkjet prints, it's advisable to spray the paper with acrylic sealer before applying mod podge. Give the spray some time to dry, haven sprayed both sides of the paper before you proceed with your project.

♦ **Tissue Paper:** There's nothing special you need to do to prepare tissue paper, but keep in mind that the thin nature of tissue makes it impossible to Mod Podge without folding. The folding on the other hand, is usually significant for the attraction of the tissue paper and further add beauty to the surface. To avoid damaging the decoupage medium, use it gently. This is because tissue is much lighter than regular paper, can easily twist around corners, and is less likely to have an outstretched surface or air pocket. Its fluffy surface gives it a painting-like appearance when compared to other types of papers.

- **Cardstock:** Cardstock is available in a wide range of design patterns and color tones, making it an excellent choice for decoupage using mod podge or any other material. Cardstock with a higher weight is a good option for 3D decoupage. Your product will appear and feel thicker with this heavier option.

- **Photographs**: Your project will always come out great when stick your photos to a decoupage. All you need do is to apply a layer of decoupage to the object's surface, overlap your photo on top, apply more glue to the layers to help the photo stick properly to the project. Decoupage can also be used to transfer pictures to other surfaces in other ways. If you're decoupaging with photographs, make sure those photographs are printed with a laser printer rather than an ink jet printer because decoupaging with an ink jet printer photograph will produce stains on your final product. To do the decoupage project, cut the needed size of paper or material. To decide on the format of your project, carry out different tests with design features. Combine little and large pieces, effectively blend the materials with nice colors to make your work more attractive.

♦ **Napkins:** Because of the nature of their pattern and how light they are, napkins are a fantastic choice for decoupage. To begin, cut out the design with your scissors before separating the napkin sheets and then apply the decoupage to its single layer.

♦ **Cut Out Photographs:** Select the pictures you want to use for your project and cut them out. Using a ruler and a pencil, take the appropriate measurements. Trim it down properly to get it fitted. Trimming it down to the appropriate size before applying Mod Podge is more preferable compared to trimming it after applying the Mod Podge. You can cut the photograph without precision first with your scissors and then precisely resize it to the desired size later with your craft knife. In a case where a white edge (excess edge) is seen around the photo, you can either cut the edge out or color it using a crayon/pen of same color as the photograph or the foundation that will be used.

Try to select photographs that are free of unnecessary complications from the start, like those that do not require much cutting or trimming. Cutting out images requires extreme focus, and the process can be tiring, especially on the eyes and hands, sitting in a particular spot with good lightening so can clearly see what you are doing. You can start with small amount of paper that you can easily cut out, get a table or tray that you can comfortably lean on. When cutting, bring the paper closer to the scissors. Using the line as your guide, twist and turn the image as you cut along the line.

♦ **<u>Organize your photos</u>**: Before applying the glue to stick the photos, make sure you are satisfied with the arrangement and position of your photos. You can arrange your photos using tweezers to get an accurate outcome.

♦ Apply Mod Podge or Decoupage Medium to each element.

# CHAPTER 7.

## INTERESTING DECOUPAGE PROJECTS.

### ♣ DECOUPAGE MARBLED HANGERS.

For this project you will need:

- Tissue paper.
- Mod Podge Matte.
- Paintbrush.
- Wooden hangers.
- Craft knife.

**Step 1:** Gently cut out tissue papers of roughly the same size as your normal house hanger with a good 2-3 inches of overhang.

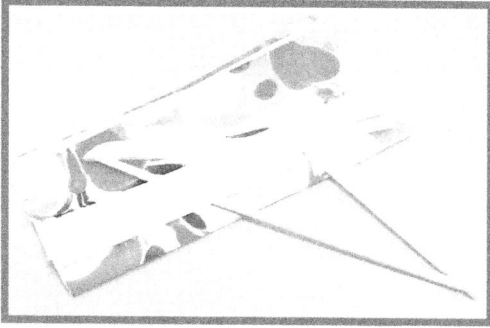

**Step 2:** Brush on a little amount of Mod Podge on a small area on the wood near the hook of the hanger. **Step 3:** Place the tissue paper on top of the wet glue and use your fingers, or a squeegee to make the paper nice and smooth and clear out wrinkles or air bubbles.

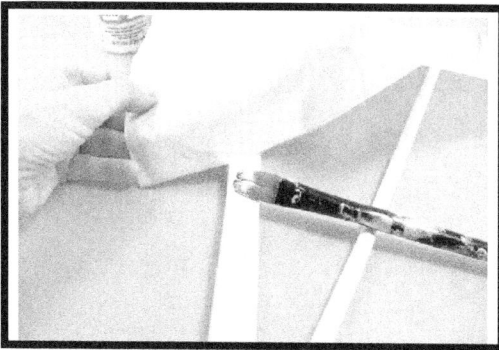

**Step 4:** A little Mod Podge is used because the wetter the application the more likely it is that you'll tear your paper while trying to smooth it down.

**Step 5:** Working in each section, glue the paper down while working from the left side to the right, leaving it for some time to dry before you pass back to the other side.

**Step 6:** Allow the paper to stick in between sets because if you work too quickly you might end up pulling the paper up back off of the surface and you will need to do that section again.

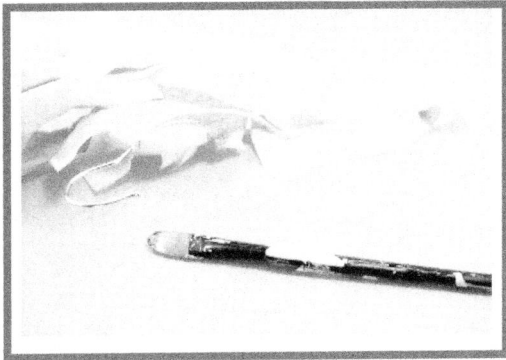

**Step 7:** When you finish the front side of the hanger, use scissors or a craft knife to create darts in the fabric over the top.

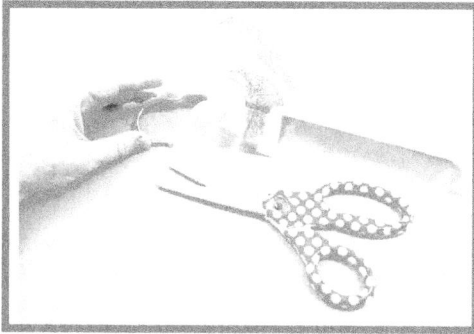

**Step 8:** Glue the pieces down onto the top of the hanger, smoothing the sections and overlapping the paper when necessary for proper coverage.

**Step 9:** In some areas, like the gap you see in the purple above, there might be a need to rip off or trim away a piece of paper that matches to discretely patch the area. Leave to completely dry.

**Step 10:** Using a very sharp craft knife or blade trim off the excess paper from the bottom and top edge of the hanger.

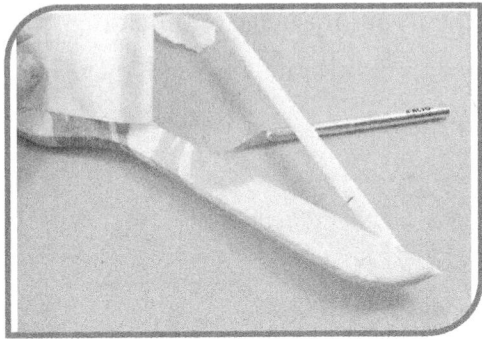

**Step 11:** After trimming, repeat the decoupage process for the backside of the hanger, trimming up the excess paper along both the top and bottom sides.

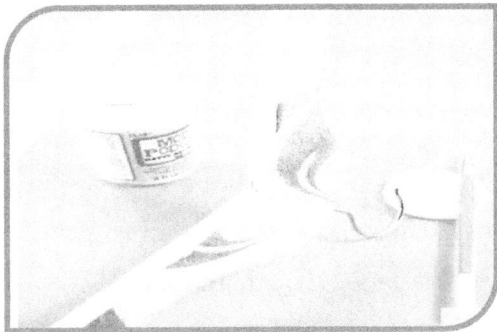

**Step 12:** To round up each hanger, add a little thin coat of Mod Podge to the surface, ensuring you cover everything properly.

**Step 13:** Leave each coat to dry completely before the next one and work in small amounts to prevent the paper from bubbling up or wrinkling beneath from the moisture.

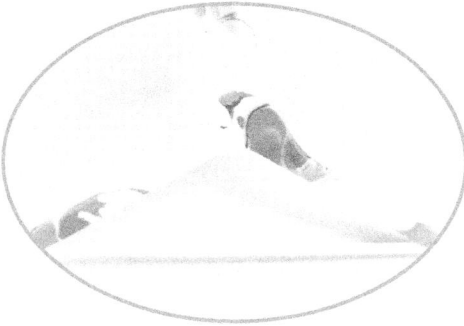

**Step 14:** When completely dry, go over each hanger again, rub your finger along the surface and find any places that catch on paper that is loose.

**Step 15:** Fix anything as required and leave to dry completely again.

# CHAPTER 8.

# IPAD CASES.

Materials needed;

- iPad case from Dollar Tree.
- Fabric Mod Podge.
- Satin Mod Podge.
- The fabric of your choice.
- Waxed paper.
- Sandpaper.
- Tools.
- Paintbrush.
- Scissors.
- Detail scissors.

**Step 1:** To arrange the fabric, paint a little layer of Mod Podge on the fabric and leave it to dry. Cover a large area enough to cover the iPad case.

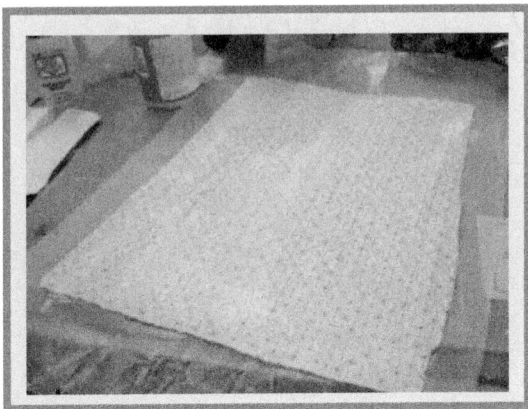

**Step 2:** Fix the iPad case on support and sand it lightly so that the Mod Podge adheres more easily, just make the surface slightly rough.

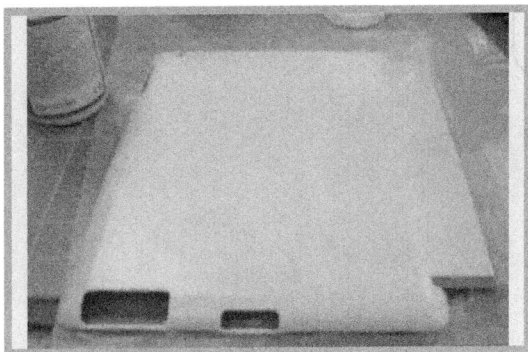

**Step 3:** Paint a mod podge layer onto the case and smoothen the fabric down on the top. Leave to dry.

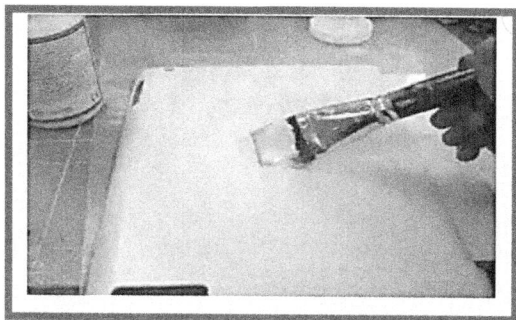

**Step 4:** With a smaller paintbrush, file the edges.

**Step 5:** Trim, apply Mod Podge, and fold over. Leave to dry.

**Step 6:** Trim the camera hole using detail scissors.

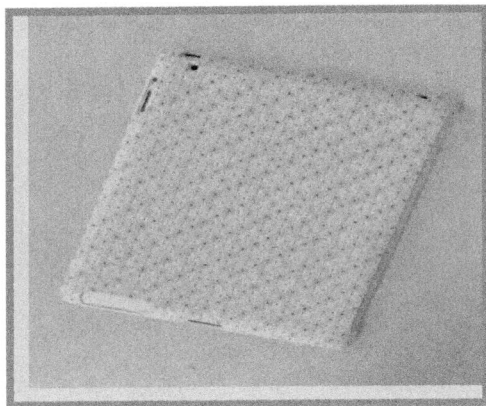

♣ <u>COASTAL MAGNETS.</u>

**Materials;**

- Marble accents.

- Glue.

- Foam brush.

- Tools.

- Scissors.

- Circle punch.

- Mod Podge Matte.

- Scrapbook paper.

- Magnets.

**Step 1:** With a circle punch, punch out circles. If a circle punch is not at your disposal, trace out the magnets on the scrapbook paper and cut it out using scissors.

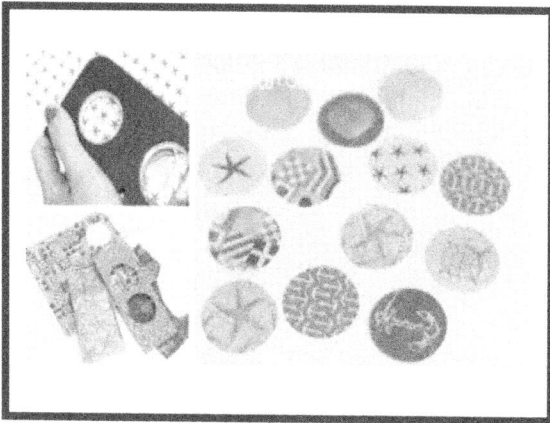

**Step 2:** Paint Mod Podge behind the marble pieces using a foam brush. Carefully place the scrap book paper above it and smoothen it down.

**Step 3:** Apply more Mod Podge behind it and leave for 20 minutes to dry.

**Step 4**: Apply a dab glue behind it and then press it firmly on your magnet.

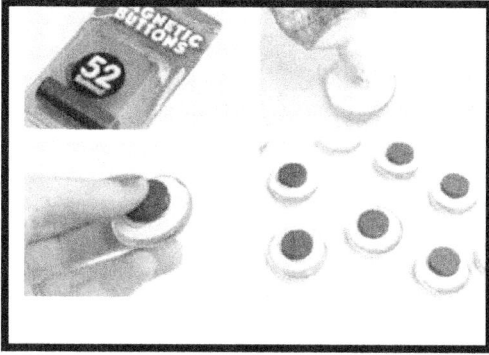

**Step 5:** Leave your magnets for several hours to dry before using or gifting.

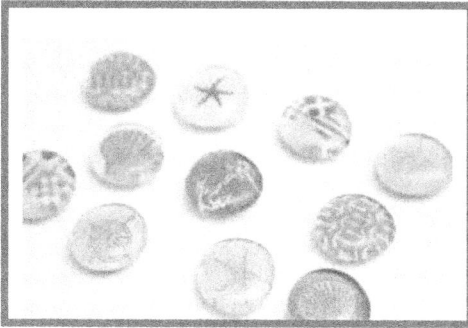

# CHAPTER 9.

## DECOUPAGE NOTEBOOK AND PENCILS COVERINGS.

*Materials:*

- Decoupage glue or water down PVA.
- Inexpensive notebooks.
- Used magazines/papers.

**Step 1:** Cut or snip out the paper. Use thin paper so that your final result will be less bulky.

**Step 2:** You can use tissue paper but you have to be careful so you do not scrunch it up and apply more layers.

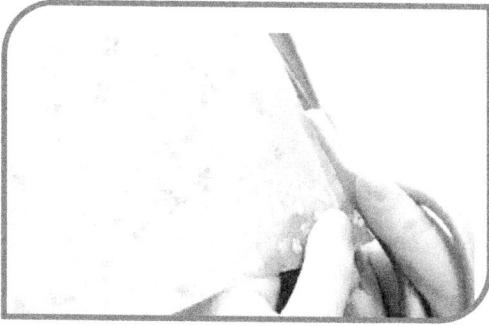

**Step 3:** Then start applying glue – apply a layer of your glue, then carefully place your paper above it. Use your brush to smoothen it down. Continue layering until you complete it.

♣ **Decoupage Pencils.**

- Use thinner decoupage paper to wrap your pencils and apply a layer of glue and attach the paper.

- Allow to dry and your decoupage pencil is ready.

# CHAPTER 10.

## AMAZING FLORAL NECKLACE.

# *Supplies;*

- Mod Podge Dimensional Magic
- FolkArt acrylic paint
- Martha Stewart Microbeads in Feldspar.
- Metal flowers or other embellishments.
- Jewelry making items like chains, loops etc.
- Mobile scanner
- Scissors.
- Pencil or pen.
- Paintbrush.
- Bangles of two inches pendant disc
- Mod Podge Gloss
- Jewelry tools.

**Step 1:** Scan your catalog on your mobile scanner.
**Step 2:** Print the design out to a piece of copy paper. If you are using a laserjet printer, you can cut out and decoupage.

**Step 3:** If you are using an inkjet printer, you can seal the paper using a clear acrylic spray sealer before decoupaging, or it might smear.

**Step 4:** Trace your pendant flat side down to your design.

**Step 5:** Cut out the paper and make sure it fits your pendant. Adjust if you need to. Set aside the paper.

**Step 6:** Paint your pendant with Blue Ribbon or any color available. Apply multiple coats and leave to dry.

**Step 7:** Apply a medium layer above the pendant. Arrange the paper above it and smoothen thoroughly.

**Step 8:** Wipe off any Mod Podge that squeezes out through the sides. Leave the pendant for 15minutes to 20 minutes to dry.

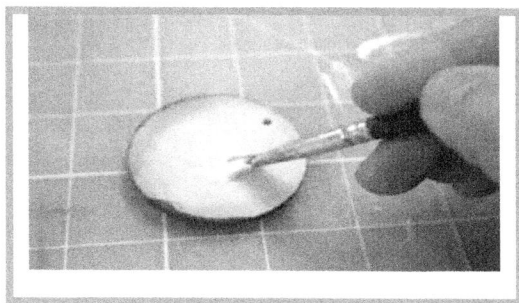

**Step 9:** Apply Mod Podge on top of the paper seal.

**Step 10:** Leave for some time to dry and then add another coat of Mod Podge.

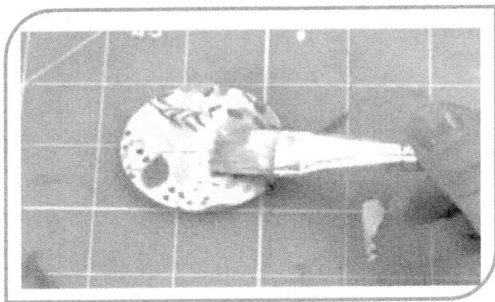

**Step 11:** Add some coordinating Martha Stewart micro-beads to add a little texture to the project.

**Step 12:** Apply Mod Podge in the areas you want the beads and sprinkle directly on top. Leave to dry.

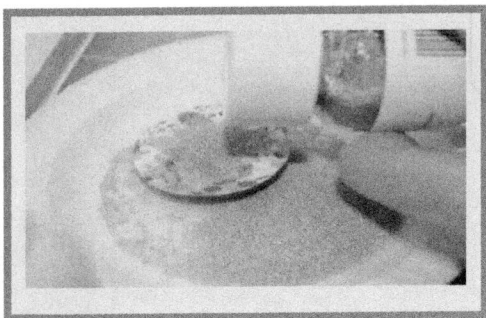

**Step 13:** Finally, apply Dimensional Magic above the pendant, right above the beads. Immediately after

applying the Dimensional Magic, stick the metal flower directly onto the pendant.

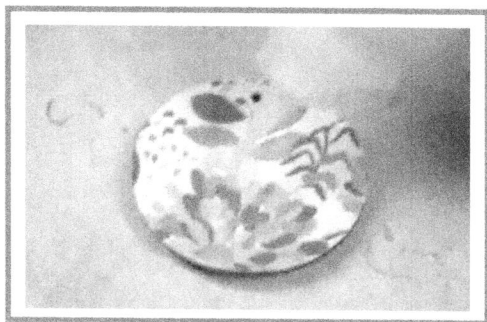

**Step 14:** The dimensional magic gets dried and will be held in position. It takes hours for dimensional magic to dry, so be patient – also leave it in a warm area. It might get cracked if it's kept in a cold room.

**Step 15:** To convert your wood pendant to a necklace, apply the jewelry findings you want.

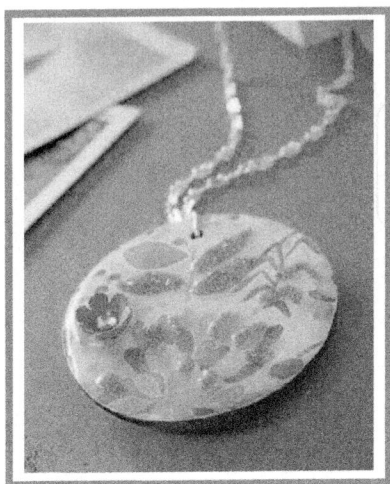

# CHAPTER 11.

## *OLD COMIC BOOK ON SLATE COASTERS.*

### *Materials Needed*

- Some pages of your old comic books.
- Ruler.
- Scissors.
- 4-inches square slate coasters.
- Mod Podge or any decoupage sealer.
- A small paintbrush.
- Clear acrylic sealer which is optional.

## ♣ Step By Step Guides.

**Step 1:** Cut the papers to about three-and-a half inches squares if you are using a slate tiles of 4-inches squares. You can also cut the paper to ½-inch in size using your ruler and scissors.

**Step 2:** Coat some amount of Mod Podge to the back of the comic book you cut out in step 1 and press the glued side on the slate tile. You need not bother about any excess glue because you can easily clean it off and it will dry off almost immediately.

**Step 3:** With your small paintbrush, apply a small amount of Mod Podge all over the comic paper you glued to the slate.

**Step 4:** After the first coating you did in step 3 dries off, you can then add more coating of Mod Podge. You can as well coat with a clear acrylic sealer to make the coaster waterproof.

## ♣ <u>Plate Decoupage.</u>

### <u>Materials Needed:</u>

- Clear glass or plastic plates

- Mod Podge in your desired finish.
- Paintbrush.
- Patterned paper or cardstock.

- Pencil.

- Scissors.

## ♣ <u>Step By Step Guides.</u>

<u>Step 1:</u> Wash the front and back of each glass plate, and let dry completely. Use rubbing alcohol to remove any soap or oils.

<u>Step 2:</u> Measure and cut your paper/fabric to fit your plate size;

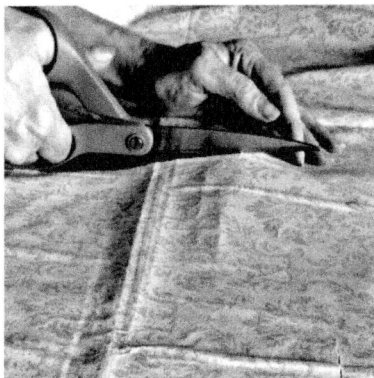

<u>Step 3:</u> coat the back of your plate with Mod podge using the foam brush;

<u>Step 4:</u> place your fabric/paper on the center of the plate with the printed part of the fabric/paper faced

down and smooth the edges properly to remove any air bubbles.

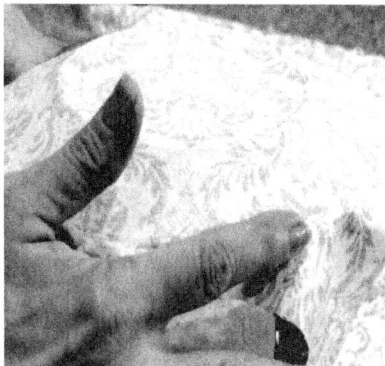

**Step 5:** Apply another layer of Mod Podge on the fabric/paper that is glued to the plate;

**Step 6:** place the glued plate (s) on a standing surface for the glue to dry properly. You can leave it for hours or a day.

**Step 7:** Trim the edges to remove excess fabric with a pair of sharp scissors

**Step 8:** You can apply acrylic spray on the plate to protect its look.

♣ <u>Book Shelf Decoupage.</u>

<u>Materials Needed</u>

- Wooden shelf

- Scissors
- Tape measure
- Mod Podge Matte
- Mod Podge Hard Coat
- Fabric
- Sanding & priming supplies
- Sponge brush
- Brayer

## ♣ <u>Step By Step Guides.</u>

<u>**Step 1.**</u> The first most important thing to do after gathering your material is to smoothen your wood (to avoid rough edges).

<u>**Step 2:**</u> Cut out enough fabric that will cover the size of the wood you are using for the shelf with half an inch on the ends.

You also need an open ends on the shorter side of the wood and some little extra on the long side so as to enable you fold leftover fabric to the edge that will be facing the wall where the shelf will be nailed to.

**Step 3:** Apply your **Mod Podge** to one side of the wood you are using for the shelf.

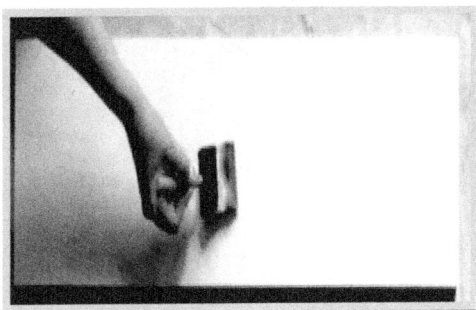

Gently fix the fabric so it sticks firmly on the wood and leave an extra half inch of fabric hanging out from the first end.

**Step 4:** Apply Mod Podge to the front edge of the wood and gently fold your leftover fabric over it. Use your hand to smooth it into place tightly.

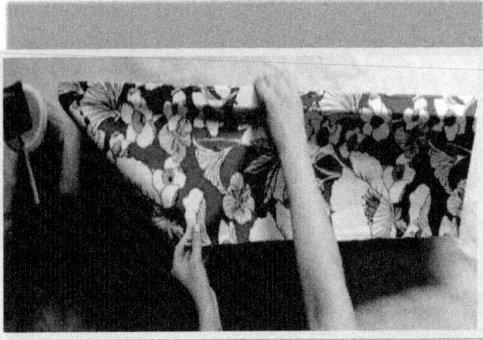

**Step 5:** Apply Mod Podge on the other side of the wood and fix the fabric on it firmly. There should be about a half inch of extra fabric on both ends of your fabric.

**Step 6:** Re-apply the Mod Podge all over the outer side of the fabric.

Then use a brayer to smoothen the Mod Podge all over the fabric. Do this until the entire shelf is completely covered with Mod Podge and allow it to dry properly.

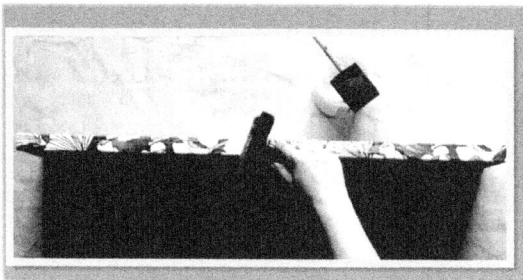

**Step 7:** In this step, you may either leave your end product at step 6 or apply Mod Podge hard coat and give it some days to dry properly before hanging it on the wall.

# CHAPTER 12.

# WINE BOTTLE DECOUPAGE.

## Materials Needed.

- ◆ Empty wine bottle.
- ◆ Mod Podge.
- ◆ Q-tip or scissors or razor blade.
- ◆ Pattern tissue paper.
- ◆ Paint brush.

**Step 1:** Remove the label on the bottle and clean very well to remove dirts;

**Step 2:** Use multi-surface paint to cover the entire bottle. Allow it to dry and re-coat it again.

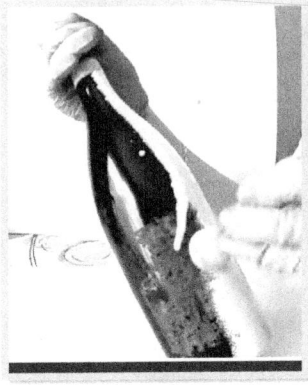

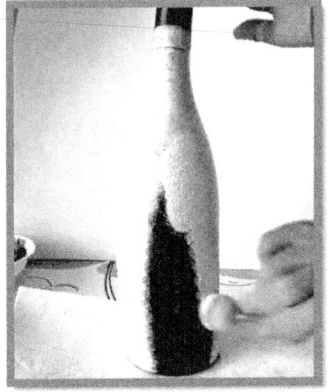

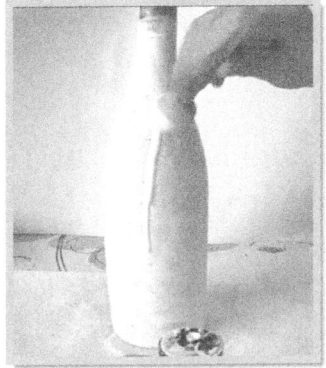

**Step 3:** Take your patterned paper napkin and remove the top layer.

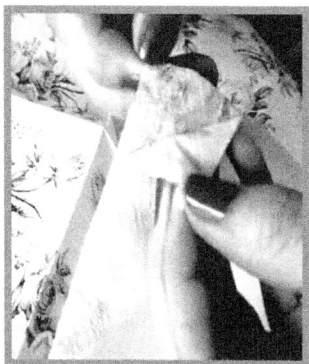

**Step 4:** Use a Q-tip soak in water to cut out the pattern on your paper napkin.

Do this until you get the desired numbers that will cover the bottle.

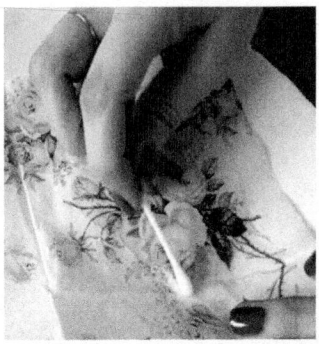

**Step 5:** Orderly arrange your flowers according to the way you want to glue them to the bottle.

**Step 6:** Glue the flowers to the bottle one by one until the entire flower is exhausted. For every flower you gum to the bottle always apply the glue on its top so it will stick firmly.

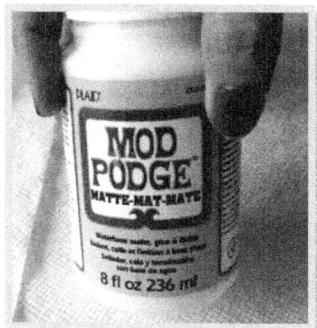

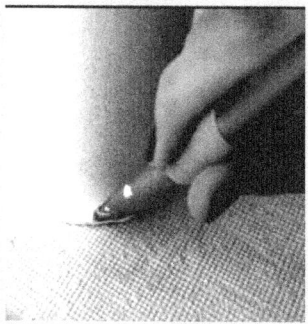

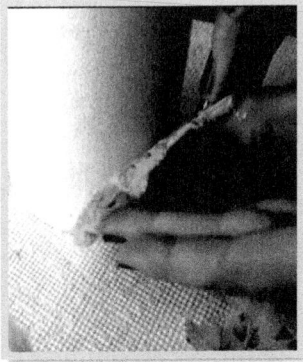

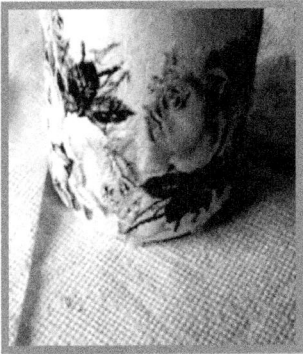

**Step 7:** Print your phrase in a mirror form horizontally and glue it with your mod podge to the top of the bottle then allow it to dry. Note.. This step is optional. You may not to write a text on your bottle.

**Step 8:** Rub the top layer of the glued paper off with water to reveal your write up and apply your mod podge on it.

♣ **Lamp Shade Decoupage.**

**Materials Needed.**

- ◆ Lamp shade.
- ◆ Mod Podge gloss.
- ◆ Paint brush.
- ◆ 1 yard of Cotton fabric.
- ◆ Scissors.
- ◆ Pen/pencil.

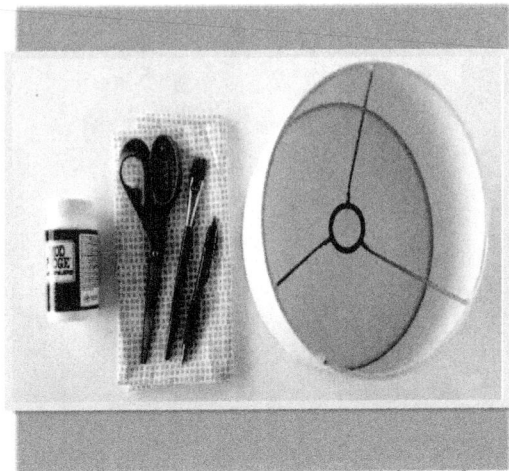

**Step 1:** In order for you to get the best result from your work, you should iron the fabric before using it, to remove folds or you can iron the fabric after you have cut it into your desired size.

**Step 2:** Spread your fabric on a flat surface with the backside faced up. Put the edge of the lampshade at one end of the fabric; leave enough space up and down the fabric because the lampshade pattern will curve round.

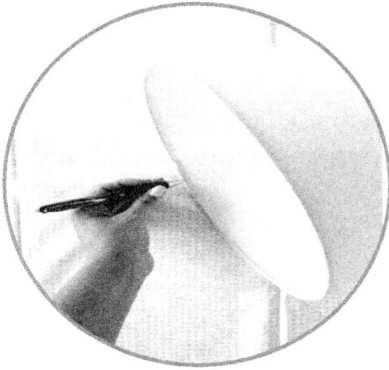

**Step 3:** Trace, using a pencil form up to down of the lampshade and roll it over the fabric till it gets to the edge again. You need not worry about having an exact trace because you aren't cutting along the lines. It's just to get a frame point to cut.

**Step 4:** Haven done step 3 above, cut out your pattern and leave about 1inch space around the marks to enable you fold the left over fabric to the edge of the lampshade.

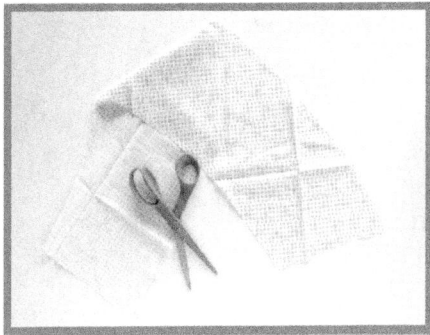

**Step 5:** Use the large paint brush to apply your mod podge gloss glue all over the lampshade, stick the fabric to the glue and smoothen the fabric with your

hands. Do this section by section until the lampshade is totally covered with the fabric.

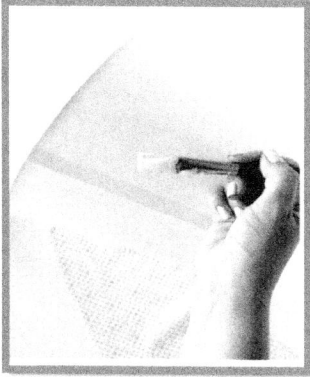

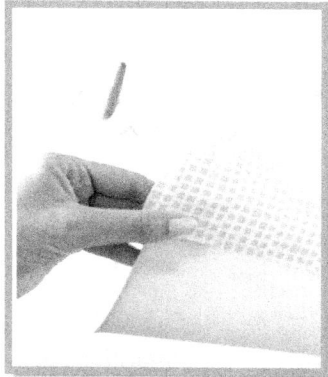

**Step 6:** Where the both ends of the fabric meets, fold one side over half an inch and glue it on top the other end to get a clean closure.

**Step 7:** Fold the remaining ends of the fabric both at the top and bottom of the lampshade and stick it

inside. It there is any bar (that joins the lamp to the base) inside the lampshade, you can slit the fabric with scissors and fold the fabric neatly around it.

Then allow it to dry totally.

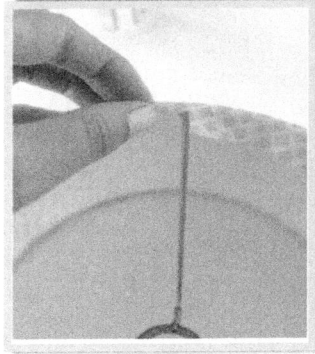

# CHAPTER 13.

## MARBLE HANGER.

### *Materials Needed:*

- ♦ Wooden hangers
- ♦ Tissue paper
- ♦ Mod Podge Matte
- ♦ Paintbrush
- ♦ Craft knife

## ♣ Step By Step Guides.

**Step 1:** Cut your tissue paper same size with the hanger you are using with an extra inches.

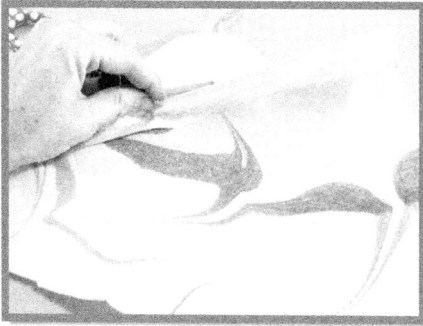

**Step 2:** Using your brush, apply small quantity of mod podge all over the wooden part of the hanger.

Place the tissue paper on the wet glue, smoothen the surface with your fingers or squeegee to remove wrinkles and air bubbles. Do this on both sides of the hanger, however ensure to let one part dry up properly before turning over to the other side.

*Note:* do not apply too much glue to the wood to avoid tearing up the tissue paper.

**Step 3:** After covering the front side of your hanger, make darts on the fabric using a scissors or craft knife along the top of the wood.

**Step 4:** Glue the dart pieces to the top of the hanger. Smoothen every section and overlap the tissue paper when necessary for proper coverage and allow to dry well.

**Step 5:** Trim off all excess tissue paper at the base and top edge of the hanger using a craft knife or new razor blade.

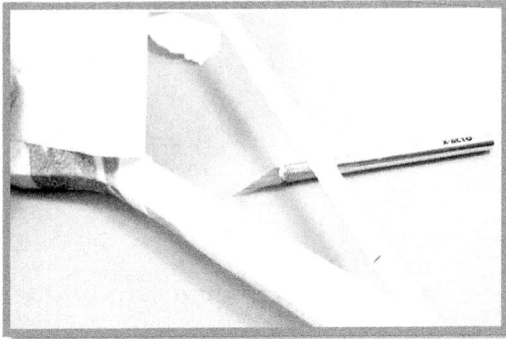

**Step 6:** Seal up all edges of the hanger using the mod podge and brush to prevent peel off while using the hanger.

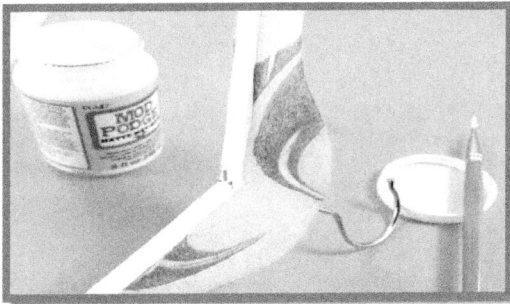

**Step 7:** finally, coat in a few layer of Mod podge on the hanger to prevent damage from moisture and allow to dry properly.

# CHAPTER 14.

## SNOWFLAKE VOTIVES DECOUPAGE.

- 1 sheet of laser-cut paper.
- Mod Podge Matte.
- Food coloring.
- Water.
- Small bowl.
- Paint brush.
- Sponge brush.
- Waxed paper.
- Glass candle jar.

## ♣ Step By Step Guides.

**Step 1:** Prepare the laser cut paper; lay it on a waxed paper, mix some drops of food coloring and water together and paint it on the paper. Allow it dry out.

**Step 2:** Cut the sheet into equal half once it dries up.

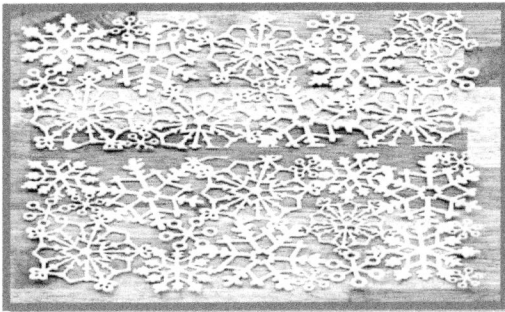

**Step 3:** Paint some amount of mod podge around the vase, wrap one of the sheets around the candle vase to get the appropriate length that can cover the vase leaving a enough extra paper to overlap.

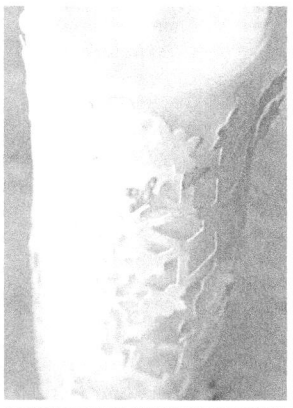

**Step 4:** Firmly stick your paper to the candle vase, add little mod podge to any overlap paper.

**Step 5:** Coat in some mod podge after wrapping the paper for a lasting stick.

# CHAPTER 15.

## GARDEN POTS DECOUPAGE.

*Materials Needed:*

- ◆ Terracotta Pots.
- ◆ Paper Napkins.
- ◆ Mod Podge.
- ◆ Outdoor Paint.
- ◆ Foam Brush.

♣ **Step By Step Guides.**

**Step 1:** Coat the terracotta pot using the white deco-art paint. Allow to dry after coating.

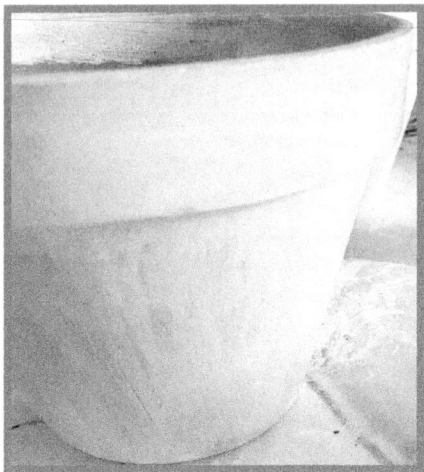

**Step 2:** Unfold the nakpin by separating the layers because you will be needing only the printed layer.

**Step 3:** Cut out the flowery design from the paper and glue to the pot. You can still use the nakpin without cutting out the design though.

**Step 4:** Coat in some amount of mod podge to the glued nakpin flower cut outs. Continue adding the design till the entire pot is covered.

## ♣ How To Use A Full Paper Nakpin For Garden Pot Decoupage.

**Step 1:** Peel out the top layer of the nakpin and cut into 4 equal squares.

**Step 2:** Coat the pot with mod podge section by section and lightly glue the napkin to the pot.
Do this repeatedly until the entire pot is covered and smoothen with your fingers to remove every bubbles and wrinkles.

## DOILY WALL ART DECOUPAGE.

♣ **Materials Needed**

- ◆ Canvas.
- ◆ Doily.
- ◆ Mod Podge for painting and some fabrics.
- ◆ FolkArt paint.
- ◆ Scrapbook paper.
- ◆ Craft knife and mat.
- ◆ Paint brush.

♣ **Step By Step Guide.**

**Step 1:** Spread a reasonable quantity of mod podge across the canvas;

**Step 2:** Lay your scrapbook paper on the coated canvas, smooth it properly, wipe off excess mod podge and allow to dry up.

**Step 3:** Add the fabric mod podge to glue your doily against the paper.

**Step 4:** Properly roll out the doily on the canvas using a brayer.

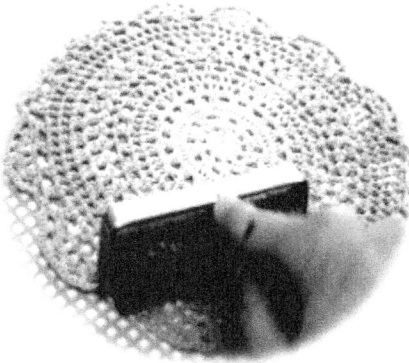

# CHAPTER 16.

## CONCLUSION.

The art of decoupage is surprisingly easy to perform by hand. Decoupage, despite the fact that the end item may resemble a painted work of art, is the process of flawlessly adhering paper crafts or other materials to a project. Decoupage is the art of decorating anything with a variety of papers and techniques.

There is no one thing that is the perfect surface to use or to decoupage on; it's all about creativity and experimenting. You may either make your own decoupage or buy it in a variety of forms. Decoupage is a method that focuses on modifying and repurposing things that you already own. In the areas below, you'll find a variety of adhesives, supplies, ideas, and suggestions for all of your decoupage projects.